THE HOLY LAND

PICTORIAL GUIDE AND SOUVENIR
by *Bob Baseman*

Published by Palphot Ltd.

Contents

Photographers: L. Borodolin, N. Follberg, Garo Nalbandian, D. Rubinger, R. Nowitz, S. Mendra, J. Sahar, D. Tal and M. Haramati, H. Krackenberger.

ISBN 965–280–069–4

Introduction

A visit to the Holy Land is a constant shuttle between the rich texture of the past and the reality of a dynamic present-day miracle – the State of Israel. No country of its size offers the visitor such a wealth of images, memories and contrasts. The stately desolation of the Judean desert, the lush patchwork of the Jezreel Valley, the calming blue depths of the Sea of Galilee, the hustle of Tel-Aviv, and the sanctity of Jerusalem are all within comfortable travelling distance of each other.

That this seemingly insignificant mass of dust-chaffed rock could become the stage for some of man's most stirring moments is the result of a remarkable interplay between Divine Will, geographical situation and one people's dogged trek through history.

The Holy Land is sacred not only by virtue of those Biblical events which have occurred within its borders, but also in light of the special relationship between God, the children of Israel and the Land (Zec. 2, 12; Isaiah 14, 2; Ez. 11, 17) which has culminated in the present State of Israel.

One need only stand at the summit of Megiddo (Armageddon) and look across the Jezreel Valley to feel the tingling sweep both of this country's past and of its future destiny. It is a hot day with the sun beating down strongly. An occasional breeze provides a moment's reprieve from the heat. The guide's voice is suddenly drowned out by an airplane streaking overhead. Before you is spread modern Israel, the numerous agricultural collectives with their cottonfields and fishponds. Suddenly it dawns upon you. Underneath is Solomon's Chariot city! Right of you, atop Gilboa, Saul and Jonathan were slain by the Philistines, on its slopes Gideon and his 300 set out against the Midianites. Ahead of you is Moreh where the Midianites camped, not far from Shunem where two centuries later the Philistines encamped before the defeat of Saul. On the

other side of that same hill Moreh lies Nain, where Jesus raised the widow's son to life (Luke 7, 11). To its left is the beautifully rounded Tabor, where Deborah and Barak defeated the Canaanites; even further left stretches the long ridge of the Lower Galilee. Wedged in a vale between the hills is Nazareth, the modest town where Jesus grew up. This valley so stained by battle in the past is slated in Revelations 16, 16 for the final battle of Armageddon.

Before we set out on our pictorial trip throughout the Holy Land, a painless geography lesson is in order. This will help us understand a simple fact: the geography of Israel dictates the strategies of war, commerce and the location of biblically important sites. It is no wonder that so many happenings took place near Megiddo, for it and the Jezreel valley lie right on one of the world's most important highways – the Via Maris or coastal route. This road connected the two greatest rivals in the ancient world, Egypt and Mesopotamia, who depending upon the political climate of the day, would utilize this route either for military campaigns or peaceful commerce. Megiddo guarded a strategic pass along this route and was subsequently called upon numerous times to block an invading force. Neither the Egyptians nor the Mesopotamians (Assyrians or Babylonians) were anxious to fight battles on their own territory, but rather on some ground between themselves and their rival. Thus the military and commercial significance of the Holy Land lies in the fact that a land force crossing Egypt to Mesopotamia, or in a larger sense from *Africa* to *Asia*, must pass through Israel. As you see, we are lying on a primary world route.

The Via Maris, as well as other routes in the Holy Land, had to accommodate itself to the specific rugged landscape of Israel. These same factors, the deserts, hills, valleys and dunes, still influence the highway building of today; no wonder the present day roads follow closely, if not identically, the classical routes. The terrain can be divided into three north-south strips: the coastal plain, the central mountains and the Jordan River valley.

Coastal Plain

The coastal plain stretches in gentle crescent along the Mediterranean for about 260 miles from the Suez Canal to the Ladder of Tyre on the Israel-Lebanese border. Throughout history this plain has been the traditional corridor from Israel down to Egypt and an important component of the Via Maris. Now a fertile area with citrus groves and large population centres (Gaza, Ashkelon, Ashdod, Jaffa, Tel-Aviv, Haifa and Acre), it has also been an area of desolation through long stretches of history due to the razing of forests during wars, subsequent loss of topsoil and the accumulation of dunes with a resultant poor run-off.

There is only one principal obstruction along the entire plain: Mount Carmel (1600 feet high), which juts out from inland into the sea and blocks the route at Haifa. While a modern road passes beneath the Carmel promontory in a narrow strip along the beach, ancient travellers wishing to continue north-east to Mesopotamia had to skirt around the entire mountain or seek a pass through it. Such a pass was at Megiddo.

Central Mountains

Passing inland, we come to the central mountain chain of Israel, the biblical heartland of Judea and Samaria. In Jesus' time, Jerusalem and the South were part of Judea, while the area around Shechem was Samaritan country. The mountains here are not sharpened peaks, but rather gracefully rounded hills 2000 feet high. Soil erosion has exposed the grey limestone boulders except in those areas painstakingly terraced by the Arab farmers or afforested by the government. This was Joshua's chief area of conquest after he came up from Jericho, and was Israel's principal area of settlement throughout most of her history. Such important cities as Hebron, Bethlehem, Jerusalem, Bethel, Shilo and Shechem are located here in the heights, and strangely enough along the same Biblical mountain highway.

It is no coincidence that this vital north-south mountain highway is virtually unchanged over 4000 years, but rather a reality dictated by the geography of the hills themselves. The central

Part of the Madeba mosaic map of the Holy Land from the 6th Century A.D. with Jerusalem in the centre. The Greek name places are those of settlements mentioned in the Bible.

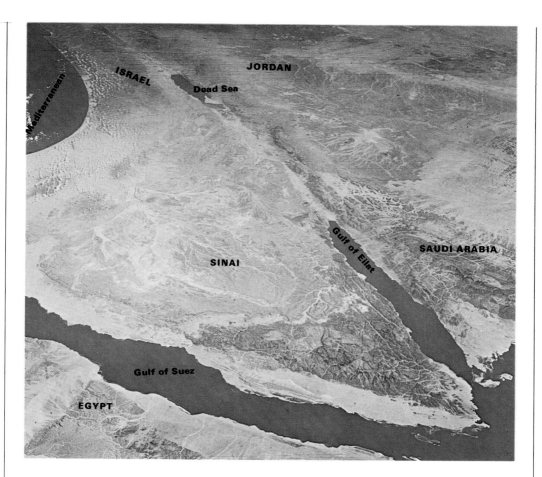

range is comprised of a ridge stretching north to south with many side branches sloping either west to the Mediterranean coast or east to the Jordan Valley. A traveller proceeding by foot along the length of the mountains would find it extremely difficult to negotiate the ups and downs of the side branches, their hills and valleys. He would be forced to travel along the very top of the central ridge. And thus, if the central mountains are the backbone and ribs of the country, then travelling the ancient mountain road is actually "tickling the spine" of Israel. Either side of this route leads downward through rough hilly terrain. This mountain route actually lies on the watershed of Israel; rain falling on the one side of the roadway flows down towards the Mediterranean, and on the other side to the Jordan.

Galilee

The northern extension of the mountain chain is a rather disjointed area of broken hills and valleys whose general elongated form has been altered by earthquake activities over the ages. This is the Galilee region. A secluded area with difficult accessibility, it was often the home of tough mountain folk as the natives of Nazareth must have been, or a refuge where guerillas could organize, as did Josephus against the Romans. Galilee is divided from the rest of the country to the south by a wide valley stretching from the Mediterranean coast to the Jordan. Because this valley is practically the only break through the mountains, it

The Holy Land with the Sinai peninsula in the foreground: view from a satellite.

became an important part of the Via Maris on the coastal plain skirting Mt. Carmel and emerging through the pass of Megiddo. Megiddo guards the western approach to the long Jezreel Valley.

Jordan River Valley

Travelling from Jerusalem to Galilee did not necessarily mean taking the mountain route by Shechem and across the Jezreel Valley. Descending 15 miles to the east of Jerusalem one enters the Jordan River valley and its most illustrious settlement Jericho, the world's oldest city. The Jordan valley is part of a much larger geotetonic trough – the Syrian-African rift valley – which stretches from Syria into Central Africa. On the shores of the Dead Sea, not far from Jericho, is the world's lowest point, 1292 feet below sea level. Capernaum and the Sea of Galilee, located in the same trough some 80 miles to the north, are 600 feet below sea level. Flowing down the center of this trough from Mt. Hermon – Israel's northernmost point – to the Dead Sea is the Jordan River, site of Jesus' Baptism and chief supplier of water for Israel's massive irrigation projects. Taking this route from Galilee to avoid Samaria, would be to enter Jerusalem by the side door, so to speak. Jesus used both the mountain and Jordan routes to come to Jerusalem from Galilee (Luke, 18:31–34; Luke, 17:11).

5

Jerusalem

Jerusalem of Gold, Jerusalem the Holy – if only the cruelties of history had not made such a travesty of her name – the city of Peace. The violent tones of destruction and rebuilding, conquest and reconquest, are but rhythmed background to the strained motifs of three faiths: To Moslems it is El-Kuds, Islam's third holiest site where the prophet Mohammed ascended skyward. To Jews, Yerushalaim is the Crown of Israel, Israel's eternal capital, site of the Temple, seat of David and chosen city of God. "If I forget thee O' Jerusalem, may my right hand lose its cunning," has become the spiritual dictum, expressing one people's devotion to its capital. Christians too treasure Jerusalem, for here Jesus walked, taught and suffered through the final passion designed to redeem Mankind from sin.

On the following pages we shall retrace our steps through Jerusalem but first let us scan its remarkable history.

Jerusalem, first mentioned in Genesis (14:18), was a Jebusite city during Abraham's time. Moriah, site of Abraham's sacrifice of Isaac, is traditionally identifed with Zion, the Temple Mount.

In 1000 B.C. David established his capital here and brought the Ark to Mt. Moriah. Jerusalem, wedged between Benjamin and Judah, was to unite the tribes into one strong kingdom. After the death of King Solomon, builder of the First Temple, the kingdom was split into Israel and Judah.

The First Temple Period ended with the Temple's destruction by Nebuchadnezzar of Babylon in 587 and the Babylonian exile of Jerusalem's elite until their return in 538 B.C. to rebuild the city and Temple. Jerusalem's conquest by Alexander the Great in 332 B.C. ushered in the forces of Hellenization. Jewish rule was regained in 165 B.C. after the Maccabean revolt. This dynasty was finally usurped by the Roman-appointed Jew, Herod, in 37 B.C.

Herod's great construction works can be seen in part till this day, though most of the city and its Temple were destroyed by the Romans in 70 A.D. The city was razed once more after the failure of the Bar Kochba revolt in 135 A.D. heralding in an entirely pagan city, Aelia Capitolina, in Jerusalem's place.

Byzantine rule succeeded Roman rule in the late 3rd century. The spread of Christianity enhanced the Holy Land's position in the Byzantine world, and it became a flourishing centre for both settlers and monastics. Jerusalem fell to the Persians and the forces of Islam in 613 and 638 respectively. The Ummayad and Abassid Caliphs were driven out by the Crusaders in 1055 only to be usurped by the Egyptian Mameluks in 1250, who were succeeded by the Turks in 1517. The city lay in neglect for 400 years until 1917. This marks the beginning of the British Mandate of Palestine. The War of Independence in 1948 resulted in the city's division into Jordanian and Israeli sectors. The Six Day War brought about the reunification of the city under the Israeli flag.

The Old City of Jerusalem seen from the Mount of Olives

The Dome of the Rock

The focal point of Jerusalem both today and at the time of Jesus was Mt. Moriah. Today the site is the home of the impressive and austere Dome of the Rock. It is set on the actual bedrock of the highest point of the Temple Mount on the eastern hill. This superb structure was built by the Moslem Caliph Abd el-Malik in the year 691 A.D. That makes it nearly 1300 years old. When it was being constructed there were still many Byzantine artisans living in the city. This explains the interesting juxtaposition of Arabesque script on Byzantine-styled mosaics. The eight-sided structure is very similar in form and artistic origin to St. Peter's house at Capernaum. Votive offerings and small shrines from Moslem rulers throughout the centuries stud the entire plaza area. Renovated in the 1960's, the former cast iron dome was replaced by one of zinc-aluminium alloy 1/6 of the weight! Inside the building is seen the hallowed rock itself. According to Moslem tradition it is from this point that Mohammed leapt skywards. To the Jew this rock has a significance stretching at least 2000 years before Mohammed, for it was here on Mt. Moriah that Abraham offered his only son Isaac as a sacrifice (Gen. 22:2). It was this same site that David purchased from Ornan the Jebusite in 1000 B.C. as a home for the Ark of the Covenant. But it was up to King Solomon to finally build God's Temple, destined to make Jerusalem Judaism's focal point to this day. Most biblical authorities identify this rock with the Holy of Holies.

Top: The Dome of the Rock, bird's eye view.
Right: Interior of the Dome of the Rock

The Western Wall

The Western (Wailing) Wall was not actually part of the Temple. Biblical Jerusalem was built on two hills: the eastern Moriah, and the western. Between them was a valley which has since been filled in by the debris of the destroyed Temple and was situated where the present plaza in front of the Western Wall is located. There is yet another reason why Moriah has lost its hilly appearance. The Western Wall is actually a retaining wall built by Herod in 20 B.C. surrounding the entire eastern hill, raised with fill to form a flat plateau the level of Moriah's summit (the threshing floor of Ornan). It was on this elevated plaza that the Temple stood at Jesus' time.
Ever since the destruction of the Second Temple, Jews have gathered in pilgrimage and in prayer at the Western Wall. Its cracks are filled with hastily written prayers for the speedy recovery of the sick, for the Peace of Jerusalem and the coming of the Messiah. Orthodox Jews will approach no closer to the Temple than this, for fear of encroaching upon the sacred precincts of the defiled and destroyed Temple.

The Excavations at the Wall

Since 1968, extensive excavations have been undertaken in the vicinity of the Temple Mount with the intention of disclosing more of Jerusalem's past, especially the Second Temple period. To the left we see the south-west corner of Herod's retaining wall. While the small stones on top are from a recent period, the large masonry extending down the lower two-thirds of the wall dates from Herod's time. Thousands of coins from all periods – Maccabean, Herodian, Roman, Byzantine, Early Arab and Crusader – have been unearthed. One interesting discovery plucked

The Western Wall during a festival
from the rubble beneath this corner was a niched cornice from the Herodian period inscribed "to the place of the trumpeting". We have found the very place where the Temple priests would herald in the Holydays and Sabbath.

The silver dome belongs to the El Aqsa Mosque, a chief component, along with the Dome of the Rock, of the Moslem Compound. The third holiest mosque in Islam, it was the site of King Abdullah of Jordan's assassination in 1951, and the scene of arson by an insane person in 1969.

The archeological park along the southern wall

The Old City Walls and Gates

The Old City walls are 4,018m. long, have an average height of 12m. and are about 2.5m. thick. The present walls were constructed by Suleiman the Magnificent in 1542 along the lines of the Crusader city and in some places on even earlier foundations.

In the walls there are 34 towers and eight gates: Damascus Gate, the most ornate, where the road to Damascus used to start; the New Gate, built in 1887 to facilitate passage from the Christian Quarter to the Catholic institutions outside the wall; Jaffa Gate, originally the starting point of the road to the most important port town; Zion Gate, connecting the Armenian Quarter with Mount

Right: The Golden Gate
Centre: Inscription discovered on one of the stones of the Western Wall in the 1969 excavations reading: "And when you see this your heart shall rejoice and your bones shall flourish like an herb (Isaiah 66:14)

Below: The Damascus Gate

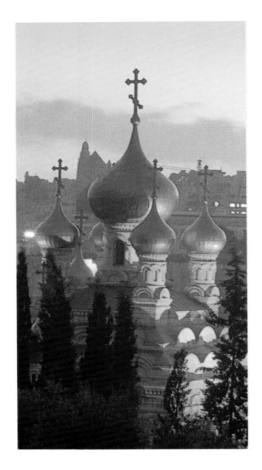

Top: The Church of St. Mary Magdalene
Top right: The Church of St. Peter in Gallicantu
The Citadel (David's Tower)

Zion; Dung Gate, nearest to the Western Wall
and through which much of the city's refuse is
taken to Kidron Valley; the Golden Gate, also
called the Gate of Mercy, which has been
closed for centuries; the Lions' Gate, or St.
Stephen's Gate, through which Israeli
paratroopers entered the City in the Six Day
War and Herod's Gate, in Hebrew called the
"Gate of Flowers".

The Citadel (David's Tower)

The Citadel, incorrectly called David's Tower,
overlooks Jaffa Gate on the western side of the
Old City. Here Herod built some of his most
impressive fortifications including the Tower of
Phasael which with its large masonry can still
be seen today just inside Jaffa gate. A climb to
the roof offers a magnificent view of the Old
City, while the lower rooms contain an
archaeological exhibition spanning Jerusalem's
long history.

The Cardo

Parts of the Cardo Maximus, the main street of
the Roman-Byzantine city, have been
discovered in archaeological excavations in the
Jewish Quarter. Byzantine and Crusader
structures have been rebuilt and included in
the design of new tourist shops which now line
the ancient way.

The Pool of Bethesda

North of the Temple Mount just inside St. Stephen's Gate lies the Pool of Bethesda or Piscina Probatica. Uncovered in 1871, the pool appears as a deep pit broken by a series of stone foundation archways upon which were built Byzantine and Crusader Churches. Used as a rain catchment pool during Herod's reign, it was part of a grandiose plan to augment Jerusalem's meagre water supply
During Jesus' time this pool was thought to have curative powers. It is here that Jesus miraculously cured the infirm man on the Sabbath (John 5:1–18).

Saint Peter in Gallicantu

St. Peter's church lies halfway down the slope between Mt. Zion and the pool of Silwan. It abounds with both tradition and some unique archaeological remains. Christian tradition places here the home of the High Priest Caiphas and Peter's thrice rejection of Jesus (John 18:27). This is also the so-called cock crowing church. A quarry in the crypt is claimed to be the Prison of Christ. The most impressive find on the grounds is an ancient hewn staircase (right) most certainly used by Christ (Neh. 12:37).

The Church of St. Anne and the Pool of Bethesda, bird's eye view

The reconstructed Byzantine Cardo

11

Hezekiah's Tunnel
Upper left: Part of the excavations of the
City of David
Left: The Silwan inscription
Opposite: Bird's eye view of the Kidron Valley
with Siloam village on the right and the Temple
Mount.

The Gihon Spring

The Gihon spring in the Kidron Valley was
ancient Jerusalem's only natural water source.
The site of Solomon's coronation, the Gihon,
also known as the Virgin's Spring, was outside
the city walls. Hezekiah in 702 B.C. built a
tunnel system which in effect brought the
water supply within the protection of the city
walls (2 Chr. 32:30) and stored the water in the
Pool of Siloah. Here Jesus cured the blind man
(John 9).
The 1500 feet long tunnel is passable to this
day. However, only the adventuresome and
sturdy are advised to wade through its
chestdeep waters.

Mount Zion

Due to a 4th century mistaken geographical
identification, Mt. Zion was attributed to its
present day site on the western hill, though in
fact Zion of the Old Testament is identical
with the city of David on the eastern hill (2
Sam. 5:7). Apparently by Jesus' time, nearly a
thousand years later, a monument to David's
tomb had migrated to the present Mt. Zion.
The tomb fell into ruin in 133 A.D., but was
accidentally rediscovered in 1158 and is
venerated to this day by Jews, Moslems and
Christians. The newly built Church of the
Dormition towers above the hill and
commemorates the tradition that here Mary,
mother of Jesus, fell into eternal sleep. On this
site stood the Byzantine church of the Hagia
Sion, the largest and principal evangelical
church in Palestine for three centuries.

The Room of the Last Supper

The Cenacle is the second floor room marking
the site of the Passover feast Jesus attended
with his disciples – The Last Supper (Mark
14:13). The present structure is a 14th century
renovation with Gothic windows and Crusader
arches.
Just as the law came forth from David's Zion
in Isaiah's time, so here did the Apostles meet
to spread the new covenant. Here Jesus
appeared before the Apostles (John 20:19–23;
22:24–29) and here, too, the Holy Ghost
descended upon the house at Pentecost (Acts
2:1–4).

Mt. Zion with the Basilica of the Dormition

The Garden Tomb

The Mount of Olives, the Church of All Nations

The Garden Tomb

The Garden Tomb, near the Damascus Gate, is acclaimed by many to be the true site of Christ's Burial and Resurrection. A nearby hillock, with a Moslem cemetery on top and a broken cistern in its rocky face, bears resemblance to a skull and this could be Golgotha/Calvary.

Discovered near the hill in 1867 was a rockhewn tomb containing two chambers. One of these has three burial places and here the Body of Jesus could have been laid. While its authenticity as Joseph of Arimathea's tomb may be disputed, the Garden Tomb, with its quiet grounds and contemplative atmosphere, is a pleasant contrast to the prodigious embellishments of nearby churches. Its cooperative and pleasant staff are available to guide visitors round the site.

The Kidron Valley

Between the Mt. of Olives and the Temple Mount lies the Kidron Valley. Here are situated some of the oldest Jewish burial tombs like the one to our left. While actually built in the Second Temple period, this monument bears the name Absalom's tomb after David's son who erected a pillar in his honour since he had no children to remember him (2 Sam. 18:18). Wayward children have often been brought here by their ruffled parents as a warning not to rebel against them, as Absalom did against David.

The Mount of Olives

For Christianity, no mountain holds more far reaching importance and sentiment than the Mt. of Olives; nowhere did Jesus spend more time during his mission in Jerusalem. Here, overlooking the Temple, he taught his disciples, on its slopes he was taken captive, and from its summit he ascended.

David came here to worship (2 Sam. 15:32). During the Second Temple period the red heifer was burnt here for the ashes of purification (Lev. 16; Heb. 9:13) and signal fires were lit at the new moon to inform the Jews of the new month's coming. Here Ezechiel viewed the heavenly chariots. In the End of Days the Lord will stand here and destroy Jerusalem, thus ushering in lasting peace (Zech. 14:1-11). It is believed that here shall begin the Resurrection of the Dead:no wonder that this is the site of the oldest and most treasured Jewish cemetery. Overlooking the Vale of Jehoshafat, these fortunates shall have a front row seat on Judgement Day (Joel 3:2).

Embellishing the mount's summit are two important Christian sites, both commemorated

by churches since Byzantine times. The Church of Eleona or Pater Noster (on left of picture) marks the spot where Jesus revealed wordly secrets to his disciples, (Matthew 24:3) and taught them "Our Father" (Luke 9).

Near Eleona stands the Crusader remains of the site of the Ascension. This small-domed structure surrounded by a circular wall (right centre) is presently a Moslem chapel. Inside is the impression of a footstep said to have been made by Jesus ascending into heaven. It was here, a Sabbath day's journey from Jerusalem, that the risen Jesus departed from his disciples, having encountered them 40 days after his crucifixion.

The Basilica and Garden of Gethsemane

In the valley of Kidron, on the Mt. of Olive's lower slopes, there stands to this day a stately grove of eight ancient olive trees. These trees and their fruit have given this site its name Gethsemane, for gat-shamna is olive press in Aramaic. The garden is well kept by the Franciscan brothers who offer pilgrims a leaf from the trees as a memento of their visit.

The focal point of the garden is the Rock of the Agony which has been covered over by the modern Church of All Nations, so called because of the world-wide contributions that enabled its construction. The church was built in a neo-classical style by the dean of Holy Land Church Architects, Antonio Barluzzi. The front facade contains a mosaic composed by C. Bargelli. It depicts Christ offering up both his and the world's sufferings.

Accompanying the mosaic is the inscription: "…with a strong cry and tears, offering up prayers and supplications was heard for his reverence" (Heb. 5,7).

Beneath the mosaic and standing upon the columns are the four evangelists: Matthew, Mark, Luke and John.

The Mount of Olives with its holy shrines and the Old City of Jerusalem in the background.

The gospel records the centrality of Gethsemane in Jesus' last days: "In the daytime he was teaching in the Temple: but at night, going out, he abode in the mount that is called Olivet (Luke 21:37). Jesus was accustomed to sojourn in this garden spot (Luke 22:39; John 18:2).

It was here at Gethsemane that Jesus came with his disciples to pray. Here he grew despondent and was tempted to find a way out, only finally to overcome the weakness of the flesh and accept the Divine Will. Betrayed by Judas, Jesus was arrested by the soldiers of the High Priest and taken away for indictment.

Below: An old olive tree in the Garden of Gethsemane

Via Dolorosa

The Via Dolorosa, or Way of Sorrow, marks the path upon which Jesus bore the cross from the praetorium (Place of Judgement) to Calvary. The oldest traditions place the Praetorium in the fortress of Antonia and Calvary at the Holy Sepulchre. The exact site of the Praetorium hinges upon the theoretical question of where Herod would have lodged while in Jerusalem. Some biblical scholars favour Herod's palace in the upper city as a probable site; nevertheless, the present route, beginning at Antonia has been fixed since the Middle Ages. Along the Way of the Cross are fourteen stations, each commemorating the events of Jesus' last walk before Crucifixion, and every Friday the Franciscans lead a procession along the way.

Procession in the Via Dolorosa

Top: Part of the pavement in the courtyard of the Antonia Fortress, the remains of which are to be found in the Convent of the Sisters of Zion. Below: The Chapel of Lithostrotos and part of the "Ecce Homo" arch in the Via Dolorosa

The Convent of the Sisters of Zion

The El Omarieh courtyard and the Convent of the Sisters of Zion mark the start of the Via Dolorosa. The convent's vaulted basement covers the remains of an ancient Roman pavement (Lithostratos) made of large flagstones, specially etched to prevent horses from slipping. It is in this entire present day complex of domed and arched buildings that the Fortress Antonia stood 2000 years ago. Within this fortress Jesus was brought before Pilate for interrogation. Scourged and mocked by Roman soldiers, he was subsequently condemned to death by Pilate at the crowd's urging. The sisters at the convent conduct very enlightening tours of the Lithostratos and offer excellent explanations of the events surrounding Jesus' crucifixion.

The Ecce Homo Arch

The Sisters of Zion purchased the Lithostratos area in 1857 under the impression that the ancient arch spanning the lane was the one from which Jesus was shown to the populace (John 19, 5). This archway, while truly quite old, actually dates from the second century A.D. Following the failure of the Bar Kochba revolt (132–135) the city was remodelled and paganized under the new name Aelia Capitolina. Though this archway is actually part of the Roman remodelling, it lies within the precincts of Antonia. It was near this spot that Pilate recited the words Ecce Homo, washed his hands and condemned Jesus to death.

Antonia Fortress

Built by Herod, the fortress towered over the Temple Mount and in Jesus' time was manned by Rome's legions. The fortress was an oblong of 450 feet by 250 feet, with four high towers, one at each corner. Its large paved inner courtyard was the Lithostratos. It is most likely

Below: The Church of the Holy Sepulchre

that within the confines of this fortress Jesus was condemned by Pilate.
Antonia's capture by Jewish Zealots in the year 67 A.D., was to mark the beginning of the Jewish revolt against Rome.

The Church of the Holy Sepulchre

The Church of the Holy Sepulchre houses the traditional site of Christ's crucifixion and burial. The site of the Church today, in the midst of the walled city, is misleading. In Jesus' time the boundary of western Jerusalem did not extend quite as far as today; Calvary was then located just outside the walls in accordance with Jewish burial tradition. Though it is now difficult to imagine the pastorality of the site in biblical days, one must keep in mind its turbulent history as well as the primary function of the early churches.
The site, apparently revered by Jesus' followers, was obliterated by a statue of Jupiter and an altar to Venus, placed there by the Emperor Hadrian in 135 A.D. Finally in 326 A.D. under the auspices of the Byzantine Emperor Constantine, the pagan shrine was removed revealing the tomb. All extraneous rock was cut away, thus enabling a large grandiose church to fit over the holy tomb and mound.

The Church of the Holy Sepulchre, the Chapel of the Angel

Consequently, the presence of the church protected and preserved the site at the cost of obscuring its original form and atmosphere. Nevertheless, one cannot help but feel the awesomeness of this monument with its high vaults, shaded corners and eastern grandeur. The Church was destroyed during the Persian invasion of 613 A.D. but was soon restored on a reduced scale only to be destroyed again in 1010 A.D. by the Caliph Hakem. The restorations of 1048 and 1149 have remained to this day, though in a bad state of repair. The church is shared by five denominations: Roman Catholics, Greeks, Copts, Ethiopian and Armenians. Each group performs separate services, maintains distinct altars and chapels and all are presently undertaking a combined programme of repair.

The edicule or housing over the tomb is divided into forward and rear sections officiated over by the Greek Orthodox and Copts respectively. The present structure was restored in the early 19th century by the Greeks. Its rich façade (right) is embellished by many lamps and ornaments in the orthodox fashion. Inside is an ante chamber containing a fragment of the rolling stone that closed the tomb. This fragment is set on a pedestal in the centre of the room. The inner room contains the Holy Sepulchre itself; all extraneous rock was removed, leaving only the plain marble slab where Christ lay.

Model of Ancient Jerusalem

Situated in the grounds of the Holyland Hotel, the Model of Ancient Jerusalem shows the grandeur of the city at the time of the Second Temple, before it was destroyed in 70 A.D. It is built on a 1:50 scale, insofar as possible using the same building materials as were employed at the time: stone, marble, wood, copper and iron. The model was designed according to the Talmud, historical sources and archeological evidence.

The Roman influence and the cultural, social and economic gap between the various groups of the population are evident. The pools – a solution to the city's water problem, the hostelries for pilgrims and the expansion north of the city, can all be clearly seen.

Partial view of the model of Jerusalem in the time of the Second Temple located in the grounds of the Holyland Hotel, Jerusalem

18

The Sanctuary of St. Lazarus at Bethany

Bethany

Heading east from Jerusalem one travels along the winding road that skirts the slopes of the Mount of Olives. Here on the eastern slope about two miles out is the present day village of El-Azarieh. One need not be a linguist to immediately see the connection between El-Azarieh and its distinguished namesake, Elazar (Hebrew for Lazarus). We have arrived at Bethany. Here was the home of Jesus' gracious friends Mary, Martha and Lazarus, as well as Simon the leper. On the Sabbath before Passover at Simon's home, Mary anointed Jesus' head with ointment and wiped his feet with her hair (John 12:3).

The modern Catholic Church of St. Lazarus stands on the site of earlier churches in Bethany not far from the tomb of Lazarus. Walking 50 feet up the pathway from the church, we come to a doorway leading down 24 steps to the traditional tomb of Lazarus. A 16th century mosque over the tomb made access for Christians impossible. The present staircase dates from 1613 and was designed to bypass the mosque, thereby enabling Christian pilgrims to view the tomb, where one of the most dramatic moments of Jesus' ministry – the Resurrection of Lazarus – occurred.

Ein Karem

Ein Karem

Located on the western slopes of the Jerusalem hills about five miles southwest of the capital's centre, Ein Karem is a tranquil pleasant village. Ein Karem means spring of the vineyard and tradition has it that this is the city of Judah referred to in Luke 1:39 where John the Baptist was born.

The village is dotted with various churches including the Franciscan Church of St. John, first built in the fifth century and whose grotto commemorates the birthplace of John. The Sisters of Zion and the Rosary Sisters have convents here, as does the Russian Ecclesiastical Mission.

The most striking church here is the Franciscan Church of the Visitation (left), presumably on the site of Zachariah's home. The church commemorates the meeting between Mary, mother of Jesus, and Elizabeth, mother of John the precursor – as reported in Luke 1, 39. "In those days Mary arose and went with haste into the hill country, to a city of Judah, and she entered the house of Zachariah and greeted Elizabeth. And when Elizabeth heard the greeting of Mary, the babe leaped in her womb; and Elizabeth was filled with the Holy Spirit, and she exclaimed with a loud cry, "Blessed are you among women, and blessed is the fruit of your womb!""

The Church of the Visitation, Ein Karem

B e t h l e h e m

Bethlehem, just off the main road six kilometres south of Jerusalem, has somehow managed to retain its quaint dignity, despite the perennial onslaught of tourists seeking some of the best Holyland bargains, Mother-of-Pearl and olivewood work being the local specialities.

Here the countryside is neatly terraced into graceful steps leading down eastward to the Judean Desert, and is carpeted with fruit-bearing olive trees. It is no wonder that Bethlehem's name is synonymous with prosperity in both Hebrew and Arabic (house of bread and house of meat respectively).

Just as the local population has been sustained throughout time by Bethlehem's agricultural productivity, so have the people of Israel and Christianity been nurtured by the events which occurred here.

Bethlehem is first mentioned in the Bible in Genesis 35:19. So Rachel died, and she was buried on the way to Ephrath (that is, Bethlehem), and Jacob set up a pillar upon her grave; it is the pillar of Rachel's tomb.

It was while gleaning barley in the fields of Bethlehem that Ruth found favor in the eyes of Boaz and was blessed by the Lord for her virtue. She was to become grandmother to the pride of Israel – King David.

Fourteen generations elapsed between David and the deportation to Babylon, and between the deportation to the birth of Jesus (Matthew 1:17). In a humble stable in Bethlehem, the drama of Jesus' mission to mankind began. And it came to pass that when they were there, her days were accomplished that she should be delivered. And she brought forth her new born son and wrapped him up in swaddling clothes and laid him in a manger (Luke 2).

The Church of the Nativity

It seems reasonable to assume that Jesus' birthplace was commonly known and revered by his followers. In 135 A.D. Bethlehem became off limits to both Jews and Judeo-Christians. Part of its paganization consisted in the birthsite being overgrown by a grove in honor of Adonis. In 330 A.D., with the Christianization of the Byzantine Empire, a splendid basilica, the Church of the Nativity, was erected on the site of the manger. Bethlehem at this period was a centre of Christian enlightenment. Here Jerome translated the Old Testament into Latin and one of the first monasteries in Palestine was built by the Roman noblewoman Paula and her daughter Eustachia.

The church was badly damaged by a Samaritan uprising (527) but was restored by the Emperor Justinian shortly thereafter. Its present form is basically that of the Justinian Church, with minor modifications. This is the only church in the Holy Land to survive the Persian invasion of 613 A.D. Legend has it that upon seeing a mosaic of the Magi dressed as Persians, the invaders decided to spare the church. The Crusaders arrived in 1099 and constructed high protective walls around the

church and adjoining monastery.

We enter the church through a small doorway (right) which receives its present form from the partial sealing of the Crusader arched entrance. The central Basilica within is decorated with hanging lamps in the Orthodox fashion, as is the manger area in the crypt beneath. The church is shared by the Greek, Latin and Armenian churches, each having separate altars. The Basilica's wall mosaics, columns and large stone floor are Crusader additions, though the mosaic floor which can still be viewed beneath, dates from Justinian's time.

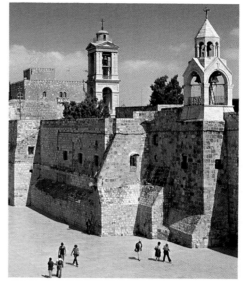

The Shepherds' Field

Descending from Bethlehem to the east, one arrives at a lower broad steppe containing the modern Arab Christian village of Beit Sahour. Here the land is flat, broad and fertile. Even today as in the days of Ruth and Boaz grain is grown here. In this pastoral surrounding "there were shepherds out in the field, keeping watch over their flock by night. And the angel of the Lord appeared to them, and the glory of the Lord shone around them, and they were filled with fear. And the angel said, 'Be not afraid; for behold, I bring you good news of great joy which will come to all the people; for to you is born this day in the city of David a saviour, who is Christ the Lord'' (Luke 2:8–11).

Right: Shepherds' Field with Bethlehem in the background
Above right: The Church of the Nativity
Panoramic view of Bethlehem

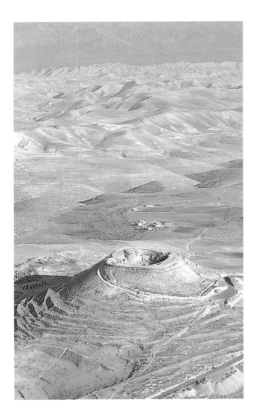

Bird's eye view of the hill of the Herodium with the Judean desert in the background

Partial view of Hebron with the Mosque of Abraham in the centre

Rachel's Tomb

Just outside Bethlehem stands the tomb of Rachel, Jacob's favorite wife, who died giving birth to Benjamin. Buried away from the family tomb in Hebron, Rachel has become the Jewish symbol of one who longs to be with his loved ones, to be back home. Rachel weeping for her children (Jer. 31:15) is said to refer to the procession of Jews deported to Babylon. Over the centuries, Jews have made pilgrimages to Rachel's tomb, seeking succour for their trials and praying for the redemption of the dispersed nation to its homeland.

Herodium

Emerging like a crater from the Judean desert, the fortress of Herodium was built by Herod the Great, to commemorate his victory over the Maccabean prince Antigones in 42 B.C. Designed to be a private pleasure palace and fortified hideaway for the debauched king, it was destined to become his grave. Most of the upper hill was man-made and faced with masonry. The hollowed out palace area above came complete with a classical Roman bathhouse.

Hebron

Hebron is one of the largest West Bank cities, with a population of 40,000, and one of the oldest, founded seven years before Zoan (the capital of Hyksos Egypt – Num. 13:22). Called also Kiryat Arba and Mamre, Hebron was an important place of encampment for Abraham, who traversed the mountains from Bethel to Beersheba. At Mamre, he built an altar to the

Lord (Gen. 13:18). Just outside of Hebron, in the Russian compound, is an ancient gnarled tree called Abraham's Oak, supposedly the site where the three angels appeared to Abraham (Gen. 18). Upon Sarah's death, Abraham bartered with Ephron the Hittite for the cave of the Machpelah. This spot was destined to become the family tomb for Abraham, Sarah, Isaac, Rebecca, Jacob and Leah.

In Hebron David ruled over Judah for seven and a half years before being anointed king over all Israel (2 Sam. 5:5). Hebron became the centre of Absalom's revolt against his father David (see Absalom's Tomb).

Hebron's chief landmark, even to this day, is the massive stone structure which Herod the Great set up around the Tomb of the Patriarchs (right centre). This site is sacred to the three great faiths of the land. A Moslem mosque and Crusader church have been superimposed on the Herodian structure. While access to the cave itself is forbidden by the Moslem custodians, visitors and worshippers of all faiths can now view the large draped cenotaphs of the patriarchs within the structure.

The Inn of the Good Samaritan

The road leading down to Jericho from Jerusalem passes through the arid Judean wilderness. At the halfway point, we come to a deserted caravan stop, used for centuries as a way station along the arduous route. This is the most likely spot for the Inn of the Good Samaritan (Luke 10:25).

Jericho

The arid climate of both Jericho and the Judean desert is due to their situation on the leeward side of the Judean mountains. Moisture-laden clouds approaching from the Mediterranean deposit their rain on the country's western regions, thus leaving a rainless strip along much of the southern Jordan Valley. Located about 820 ft. below sea level, Jericho enjoys mild winters and hot summers. A natural oasis, it has been blessed with nearby springs (2 Kings 2:19).

The key to survival in Jericho is the proper utilization of her water resources. The construction and repair of irrigation ditches, as well as a method for distributing the water among all the farmers are necessary for a viable settlement here at Jericho. Such a degree of organization appears to have first been present at Jericho by 7000 B.C., making it one of the oldest cities in the world! Even today, the extreme contrast can be seen between the desolate grey unirrigated countryside and the lush green fields of bananas, citrus and vegetables.

Old Jericho Excavations

The Tel (mound) at Jericho is one of the most extensively excavated spots in the Holy Land. Nevertheless, controversy still rages as to whether "Joshua's Walls" have actually been uncovered. Old Jericho is a "layer cake" of successively destroyed cities, each new city built on the ruins of its predecessor. The ruins gradually grow higher until a mound is formed. Archaeological dating methods have placed the first settlement (Neolithic prepottery) around 7000 B.C. These first settlers lived in mud brick huts with lime plastered floors.

Jericho seen from the Mt. of Temptation

Hisham's Palace

An ideal winter resort, Jericho was the site of a magnificent winter palace built by the Moslem Caliph Hisham whose capital was in Damascus. The restoration contains some of the most beautiful mosaics and masonry to be found in the Holy Land. The famous star was one of the former palace's second storey windows. Completed in 743 A.D., the palace was entirely destroyed by an earthquake only four years later.

Mt. of Temptation

Winding its way like an express train along the high cliffside overlooking Jericho is the Greek Orthodox Monastery of the Temptation. Returning from his baptism, Jesus was imbued with the Holy Spirit and led into the wilderness (Luke 4:1). Here he spent forty days without food, and was tempted by the Devil.

On the mount's summit lie the ruins of the Maccabean fortress, Dok where the high priest, Simon, was deceitfully killed by his son-in-law, Ptolemy, in 137 B.C. (1 Macc. 16:11).

Place of the Baptism

In those days Jesus came from Nazareth of Galilee and was baptized by John in the Jordan. And when he came out of the water, immediately he saw the heaven opened, and the Spirit descending upon him like a dove; and a voice came from heaven, 'Thou art my beloved Son; with thee I am well pleased' (Mark. 1:9).

Qumran

In 1947, a Beduin boy searching for a lost goat in the cliffs above the Dead Sea accidentally stumbled upon the Biblical discovery of the

Hisham's Palace, Jericho, mosaic floor

23

Judean desert with the Dead Sea in the background

age, the Dead Sea Scrolls. The hundreds of parchment fragments subsequently unearthed in eleven separate caves have thrown great light on the historical background of 1st century Israel. These scrolls belonged to and were written by a Jewish sect, the Essenes. Founded around 160 B.C. in reaction to growing hellenization, the Essenes sought the seclusion of the Judean Desert, where they could follow the Law more closely, and wait for the coming Messiah. They believed in two Messiahs: one, from David's line, for the Monarch, and the other, a descendant of Aaron for the high priesthood. In 68 A.D., the

The famous caves of Qumran with the excavations of the ancient settlement in the background

settlement was completely destroyed by the Romans; the scribes, seeing the approaching legions, hastily stored their scrolls in nearby caves. There these parchments remained for nearly 1900 years.

All books of the Old Testament except Esther are present, as well as apocryphal psalms, commentaries and special scrolls dealing specifically with the sect's code of ethics and beliefs.

These Old Testament manuscripts are nearly 1000 years older than previously known manuscripts. The texts are outstandingly similar to their Masoritic equivalents, showing a high degree of standardization of biblical texts before their compilation in Jamnia (Yavne) in the second century.

The Dead Sea

Nearly 1300 feet below sea level, the Dead Sea is the world's lowest point. It is actually a "dead *end*" sea, for the giant lake has no natural outlet; water entering by the Jordan, flashfloods or underground springs, can openly leave by evaporation; thus, salt concentrations build up enormously. Its high salt and mineral content (ten times that of seawater) makes the Dead Sea one of Israel's most valuable natural resources. Potash, magnesium and bromide are extracted by a process known as selective evaporation. The waters are also known for their curative powers against skin and muscle diseases.

The Spring of Ein Gedi

One of the most beautiful natural settings in Israel, Ein Gedi (spring of the kid) with its year-round waterfall and tropical vegetation contrasts with the sharp cliffs and Dead Sea shoreline. A present day kibbutz utilizes part of this local water for irrigation, and the winter harvests fetch good prices in the city markets.. It was to the caves above Ein Gedi that David fled from Saul's wrath (1 Sam. 24). Solomon extolled the fertility of this oasis in the Song of Songs 1:14.

Caves in the canyons high above Ein Gedi have revealed scrolls and letters dating from the Bar Kochba revolt in 130 A.D. In addition, a hoard of copper and ivory ritual artifacts, nearly 5000 years old, have been discovered near the fountainhead.

Masada

Rising 1400 feet above the Dead Sea shoreline, the table-top mountain of Masada stands as a tribute to Jewish resistance against Rome. The summit fortress was designed by Herod the Great as a bastion capable of withstanding a siege by his enemies. He furnished the fortress with two palaces, bathhouses, storage space and provided a water storage capacity based upon trapping nearby winter flashfloods. The fortress was garrisoned by Roman soldiers in the first century A.D. until overcome by Jewish rebels at the outbreak of the Jewish War (67 A.D.). For six years Masada served as a rebel base, where guerrilla sorties could be launched into the Judean hills. The end finally came in 73 A.D., when the Roman Tenth Legion and auxiliaries numbering ten thousand troops, staged the final assault. The nine hundred and sixty men, women and children committed mass suicide, rather than fall into Roman captivity.

Today, a cable car provides an easy approach to this once inaccessible spot. Masada, with its history, view and ruins, is one of Israel's major tourist attractions.

Right: David's waterfall at Ein Gedi
Bird's eye view of Masada with the Dead Sea in the background

25

Herodian mosaic at Masada
Left: Part of the Byzantine Church, Masada

Sodom

Deep in the Jordan Valley, beyond the Dead
Sea, lies the infernally hot city of Sodom.
Here, the yearly rainfall is less than five
inches, and summer mid-day temperatures are
well over 100 degrees Farenheit. The
whereabouts of the biblical site of Sodom is
unknown, though some believe it lies beneath
the shallow southern end of the sea.
Rising above the Dead Sea is Mt. Sodom, a
block of solid salt thrust upwards by the
tectonic quakes which have often ravished the
country. On its slope rises a pillar of salt
if you look at it long enough and let
your imagination wander a little, the figure of
a woman may be discerned. You guessed,
Lot's wife (Gen. 19:26) who looked back at the
destruction of Sodom.

Lot's wife

Arad

A true "child" of the desert, Arad is a thriving
Jewish development town in the southern part
of the Judean wilderness. It was founded by
native born urban pioneers in the early 60's
and has become a haven for new immigrants as
well. Employment is based on local desert
chemical industries. Arad also offers excellent
hotels.

*Bird's eye view of the western shore of the Dead
Sea with some of the resort hotels.*

Windsurfing on the Red Sea

The Beduin market in Beersheba

True sons of the desert, the Beduins are a semi-nomadic people, and the direct descendants of those Arab tribesmen who swept out of the Saudi Arabian Peninsula in the seventh century, spreading Islam throughout the entire Mideast.

One recurring motif in Palestine's history is the clash between local settlers and the eastern nomadic tribespeople seeking conquest or better grazing land. Joshua headed the nomadic Israelites against the Canaanites. The Israelites, once settled, had to defend themselves against Moabites, Ammonites, Midianites and Amalakites.

Each people throughout history has made the passage from nomadic hunter or grazer to settled farmer. This transformation can be seen in Israel's southern Negev area, where Beduin tribesmen have settled down into homesteads around Beersheba. They farm winter wheat especially developed for arid climates, and work as skilled tradesmen in the nearby cities of Beersheba and Arad. With permanent employment they are no longer forced to migrate seasonally to better grazing land. Nevertheless, every Thursday, the Beduins from the surrounding area flock to Beersheba for the traditional weekly market, trading produce, livestock and gossip.

King Solomon's pillars in the Timna Valley Park.

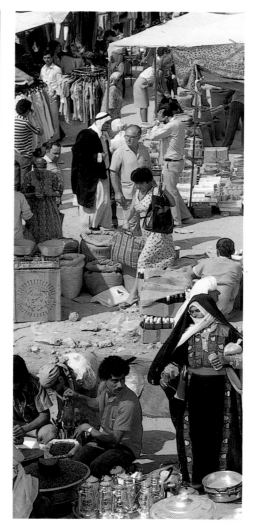

Beer Sheba, the beduin market

Eilat

The Red Sea and the Gulf of Eilat are Israel's door to Africa and Asia. The port city of Eilat is situated close to the biblical city Ezion-Geber where Solomon built a fleet of ships for trade with Ophir (Ethiopia?) (I Kings 9:26–28).

When taken by Israel Defence Forces in 1949 it was a small derelict police post and started off slowly. However, since the Sinai Campaign

A beduin winter tent made of woollen goat's hair

27

Underwater scenery in the Red Sea

and the lifting of the Egyptian naval siege on the Straits of Tiran, it has greatly developed as a port.

Because it is sunny and warm even in winter, Eilat has become a major winter resort for both Israelis and foreigners, especially Europeans who can fly there directly. Its variously priced hotels, cafes, nightclubs and restaurants and a cosmopolitan atmosphere, as-well as its magnificent underwater museum, cater to every whim.

Eilat, the resort town on the Red Sea shore

Ashkelon

Ashkelon was an important ancient post on the Via Maris. It lies 37 miles south of Tel Aviv. A Philistine centre for many centuries and staunch enemy of Israel, Ashkelon is the place where Samson slayed the thirty men (Judges 14:19) and is mentioned in David's lament over Saul's death (II Sam. 1:20) For centuries it remained an anathema to Israel, condemned successively by Jeremiah, Amos and Zephania (Jer. 47:6, Am. 1:8, Zeph. 2:4). During Hellenistic times, its inhabitants worshipped a fish goddess Dercetus. Finally captured by Jonathan the Maccabee, Ashkelon was embellished by Herod and became an important city during Roman times. The sculpture, pillars and sculpted relief to the left, are from this period. The war scene is part of the side panel of a 3rd century Roman sarcophagus uncovered in Ashkelon.

Ashkelon, ancient ruins in the National Park

Bird's eye view of Tel-Aviv with the Marina in the foreground

Tel Aviv–Jaffa

Jaffa is an ancient Canaanite city and port, traditionally named after Japhet, son of Noah. Here, according to Greek Mythology, Persius saved Andromeda from the sea dragon. The cedars from Lebanon were unloaded here and transported inland to Jerusalem for Solomon's temple (2 Chron. 2:16). From Jaffa, Jonah fled on a ship for Tarshish in his attempt to avoid God's Mission (Jonah 1:3). Over much of the Hellenistic period, Jaffa was a mixed pagan-Jewish city, with a large Greek mercantile element. It became a Jewish city after the Maccabean conquest, aroung 160 B.C., only to be lost to the Romans in 66 A.D. Its importance, though diminished in Byzantine times, was renewed during the Crusades. During the past several centuries, Jaffa was a predominantly Arab city and was the chief port of entry for pilgrims and immigrants to the Holy Land.

In 1909, a group of new Jewish settlers moved northward from immigrant-swollen Jaffa to found a new sister city, Tel Aviv. Before long, the child outgrew the parent, and Tel Aviv became the bustling business-entertainment centre of Israel. Approximately 40% of Israel's population lives within a ten mile radius of Tel Aviv. In 1950, Tel Aviv and Jaffa were united into a single municipality. Today it is a bustling western city, offering the finest in hotels, museums, concerts and shops.

St. Peter's Monastery

The Franciscan Church of St. Peter stands on the mound of Jaffa overlooking the ancient port. Walking around the restored old city of Jaffa, one can visit the traditional site of Simon the Tanner's home (Acts 10:9). Here Peter dreamt of a giant sheet holding unclean (unkosher) animals lowered from the heavens. This vision was accompanied by a voice commanding Peter to rise and kill these animals. Early Christians interpreted this dream to mean that followers of Christ need no longer observe Jewish dietary laws.

Jaffa, St. Peter's monastery

29

S a m a r i a

Travelling northwards from Jerusalem on the mountain route, one enters the historic hill country of Samaria. No part of the Holy Land offers so many biblical glimpses as this stretch of West Bank territory. Practically every village around is mentioned in the scriptures. Anatoth (Jer. 1:1); Gibeah (I Sam. 10:26); Adasa (I Macc. 7:40); Rama (Jer 40); Mizpah (Sam. 10:17–27); and Bethel (Gen. 12:9; 13:3) are all strung near the northern highway within twelve miles of Jerusalem.

Samaria is named after the capital of Israel founded by King Omri. The area was also termed the Mountains of Ephraim, for it was the inheritance granted to the tribe of Ephraim and the halftribe of Menasseh.

There are several features which distinguish Samaria from her sister Judah. While Judah is a land of canyons, steep slopes and inaccessible areas, Samaria is open hill country. Located in a central position and near international trade routes, Samaria was greatly influenced by foreign ideas and paganism. She was constantly condemned by the prophets (Amos, Isaiah).

Arab Farmer

Samaria is almost entirely Arab in both its present day population and character. Agricultural methods used during biblical times are still in use today. The hillsides are painstakingly terraced while the valleys are carefully ploughed by oxen. Recently, modern farming methods such as increased mechanization, improved strains, money crops and joined plots have been introduced with a corresponding increase in yield.

Jacob's Well

Just east of modern Nablus is Jacob's Well with the imposing though incomplete church standing above it. During Jesus' time the village was called Sychar and inhabited by Samaritans. Jesus, passing through on the way to Galilee, stopped here for a drink of water. Typifying the hatred between Samaritan and Jew, the woman refused his request. Her contempt was answered by Jesus: "Everyone who drinks of this water shall thirst again, but the water that I shall give him will become in him a spring welling up to eternal life" (John 4).

Ploughing between the olive trees in Samaria

Nablus

The largest city in Samaria. There is still a tiny community of Samaritans, but the main inhabitants are Moslem Arabs. Nablus serves as the centre for the surrounding villages and farmers from the area come here to sell their agricultural produce in the "Shuk".

Old Shechem

Nestling in the valley between the mountains of Gerizim and Ebal, Shechem (Nablus) is the first city that Abraham touched upon when he entered Canaan (Gen. 12:6). Jacob's sons massacred the city's male inhabitants (Gen. 34:25). During Joshua's time the twelve tribes took up positions on Mt. Gerizim and Ebal and a chorus of alternating curses and blessings (Josh. 8:33) rebounded from hill to hill.

With the fall of Israel, Shechem became the centre for the Samaritans but was destroyed by the Romans in the first century. In its place, a New City, Neopolis (Nablus) was established. In 636 A.D., the city fell into Moslem hands.

The Samaritans

With the fall of the House of Israel in 721 B.C., and its dispersion by the Assyrians, the countryside was repopulated by a pagan people who assumed Jewish rites and actually claimed descent from Ephraim and Menasseh. These Samaritans were never accepted as Jews by the Jewish returnees from Babylon. The refusal to allow them to partake in the Temple's reconstruction led to an irreconcilable schism between Samaritan and Jew. Their own temple on Gerizim, an afront to Jerusalem, was destroyed by John Hyrcanus in 128 B.C. A hardy people, the Samaritans withstood many attacks against them by the Romans and Byzantines and instigated a few of their own. A small remnant has survived to this day. Their 450 members reside in either Nablus or in Holon (near Tel Aviv). They accept only the Pentateuch, and their Passover is celebrated

Celebration of Passover by the Samaritans

each year on Mount Gerizim with the slaughter of the pascal lambs just as prescribed in Exodus 12, 5.

Sebastia

Sebastia in Samaria is a beautifully proportioned hill overgrown with fruit trees and vineyards. The ruins of its former cities can be seen rearing their columns through the greenery. Micha's prophecy: "And I will make Samaria as a heap of stone in the field when a vineyard is planted and will bring down the stones thereof into the valley and I will lay her foundations bare" (Micha 1:6) is a present day visual reality.

Omri established Samaria as his capital of Israel in place of Tirza (I Kings 16:15–24). Ahab and his wife Jezebel built a temple to Baal here.

Destroyed in 721, Samaria was repopulated by Babylonian settlers. The city was destroyed again by Alexander in 331 B.C. and the Maccabees in 108 B.C. Herod the Great enlarged the city and changed its name to Sebastia. Philip, Peter and John ministered here.

In the second century A.D. Sebastia became a thriving Roman city.

The Jezreel valley seen from the Balfour forest

Sebastia

Samaria's ruins include the Roman columned street and the amphitheatre.

The Jezreel Valley

The Jezreel Valley is the largest valley in Israel and cuts across the country between Galilee and Samaria. Historically it was the primary route along which armies and caravans could pass from the coastal plain into the Jordan Valley (see introduction). Situated partially below sea level and plagued by poor drainage, this now fertile valley was a malarial swamp until the early 1900's. Purchased from Arab absentee landlords in the 1920's, the swampland was reclaimed and malaria was eradicated by the new Jewish settlers. Today the Jezreel Valley is Israel's showplace of reclamative agriculture.

Nain

"Soon afterward Jesus went into a city called Nain and his disciples and a great crowd went with him. As he drew near the city, behold, a man who had died was being carried out, the only son of his mother... And he said: 'Young man I say to you, arise.' And the dead man sat up and began to speak." ('Luke 7:11).

The moslem village of Nain lies on the northern slope of the Moreh Hill on the site of Biblical Nain.

Beth Alpha

In 1926 Kibbutz workers digging an irrigation ditch in the Jezreel Valley accidentally uncovered a mosaic floor belonging to an ancient synagogue. A dated inscription places its construction during the rule of Justinian (518–527).

The central panel consists of a zodiac circle with the figure of a youth riding a horse-drawn chariot. Around the figure are the twelve signs of the zodiac, each with Hebrew inscriptions.

Mount Gilboa

This was the site of King Saul's final great battle against the Philistines in which he and three of his sons, including Jonathan, were killed.

David, in his deeply moving elegy over the fallen heroes, cursed the mountain whose summit remains barren to this day.

"Ye mountains of Gilboa,
Let there be no rain or dew upon you
Nor upsurging of the deep
For there the shield of the mighty was defiled,
The shield of Saul, not anointed with oil,

(II Sam. 1:21)

Beit Shean

The development town of Beit Shean was an important city from the Chalcolithic period until the late Middle Ages, when the city was destroyed by an earthquake.

Eighteen layers have been excavated with finds including Egyptian temples and stelae, proving that it was the administrative headquarters of Egyptian rule. Beit Shean is mentioned in the Bible when the Philistines hung the bodies of King Saul and his sons on its walls. The most impressive remains are from the Roman-

Ruins of Byzantine Beit Shean

Byzantine period when Beit Shean was a world centre for the textile trade and food production. The largest Roman theatre in the country has been uncovered here together with wide Roman streets, baths with mosaic floors and an impressive amphitheatre which has been incorporated into a national park.

Megiddo

The view from Megiddo and its strategic importance are discussed in the introduction. The tel itself consists of twenty superimposed cities, the oldest going back to 4000 B.C. The tel was finally abandoned in 400 B.C. A Canaanite city stood here around 2000 B.C., but was succeeded to by the Hyksos invaders in the 18th century B.C. The Hyksos were

Remains of the ancient harbour at Caesarea

finally subdued and Megiddo taken by the Pharaoh Thutmose in 1478 B.C. King Solomon fortified Megiddo and made it one of his chariot cities and supply centres (I Kings 4:12; 9:15; 10:26).

Two Judean kings died in battle here: Ahaziah was killed by Jehu in 847 B.C., (II Kings 9:27) and Josiah by the Pharoah Necco in 610 B.C. (II Kings 23:29).

In World War I the decisive battle in the conquest of northern Palestine by the British was fought here. General Allenby's victory earned him the title Viscount of Megiddo. Megiddo is identified with Armageddon of Revelations 16:16.

The above model gives us a good picture of how Megiddo looked at around Solomon's time. A ramp for chariots and a staircase lead up to the towered city gates. Proceeding clockwise from the gate we come to long rows of supply houses and administration buildings. The courtyards at the top are Solomon's stables. A submerged round grain silo can be seen between the courtyards. The large pit on the summit's right hand side is the entrance to the underground water tunnel which linked the inhabitants to the water source located beyond the walls. An exciting experience today is to descend the 180 feet into the pit and continue 360 feet to the spring's source.

Caesaria

Locted on the coast, Caesaria was initially a small Phoenician trading post called Straton's tower. In 25 B.C., Herod the Great built an artificial harbour and a "king size" city. This port city of Caesaria, named in honor of Augustus, was designed to link the pagan Decapolis with Rome and serve as a counterweight to Jerusalem's port of Jaffa. After Herod's death, Caesaria became the seat of the Roman government in Judea; Pontius Pilate resided here during his terms as procurator.

A bitter dispute between the local pagan and Jewish populations led to heightened Jewish resentment of Rome. With the outbreak of the Jewish revolt, Vespasian was proclaimed emperor here.

Phillip the Deacon evangelized here (Acts 8:40) and Paul was imprisoned here (Acts 23:23). The seat of government during Byzantine times, Caesaria had a population of 200,000. One famous inhabitant was Eusebeus, the first historian of the Church. Caesaria fell in 640 to the Arabs, but was retaken and fortified by the Crusaders and finally destroyed by Beybars in 1291. It is now a very popular tourist site with a fine beach, restaurant, art galleries and excavations.

Megiddo, excavations

G a l i l e e

Galilee comes from the Hebrew word "rounded", in the sense of a circuit or any other well defined region. It stretches into Lebanon to the north and into Jezreel to the south and is bounded by the Phoenician Coast and Jordan Valley.

Galilee, which was the tribal legacy of Zebulun, Issachar, and Naphtali, features an abundance of water, great fertility and separate mountainous regions, crossed by many routes.

Nazareth

Nazareth lies on the southernmost range of the Galilean hills overlooking the Jezreel Valley. Its 1230 foot height offers a spectacular view of Naboth's vineyard, Elisha's house and the Carmel of Elijah's sacrifice. Certainly all these places were well-known to the young Jesus, all within a day's hike for a healthy child raised in the clear Galilean air. He could not help but note the various peoples who criss-crossed Jezreel just beneath: Greek settlers heading east to the pagan Decapolis, Jewish pilgrims (one of which he was to become, upon reaching the age of twelve [Luke 2:42]) going up to Jerusalem, Roman legions displaying their presence and the occasional Samaritan cautious not to antagonize the local Jews. The world was buzzing around him with chatter of revolt, rumours of scandal, and the expectation of the coming Messiah. Surely, Jesus keenly perceived the tumult about him and translated this perception into worldly wisdom.

Present day Nazareth is a far cry from Jesus' hamlet yet the hills around have not moved an inch. Leading away is "the brow of the hill on which their city was built. Here Jesus was led by the indignant townsfolk to the precipice but he passed through the midst of them and went away" (Luke 4, 29).

The Church of the Annunciation

Nazareth is a large Galilean city, composed of an upper Jewish development town and the older Arab sector. Little is known of pre-Christian Nazareth. It is not mentioned in the Old Testament and only archaeological evidence points to a village inhabited during the First Temple period. Numerous silos, granaries, cisterns and oilpresses are all signs of a modest agricultural settlement.

After the failure of the Jewish revolt many Judeans resettled in Nazareth. A Christian church existed from the fourth century.

The meaning of Nazareth is as obscure as its Old Testament history, most likely it means to blossom or to gleam.

General view of Nazareth with the Church of the Annunciation

Most of the present day Faiths of the Church are well represented in Nazareth. The focal point of Nazareth is the Church of the Annunciation, situated in the city's oldest and most bustling market quarter. Here is the traditional spot where the angel Gabriel appeared before Mary to announce the birth of Jesus. This beautiful new church was completed in 1966 and replaced an earlier Franciscan church built in 1730 over older Crusader and Byzantine structures. The new structure was designed by Giovanni Musio and consists of two superimposed churches: a lower crypt preserving the Holy Grotto at the level of former churches, and an upper level which serves as the city's Catholic parish church.

Grotto of the Annunciation

The Grotto is situated at what was the extreme southern end of the ancient village. Excavations have revealed a small cistern with inscribed plastered stones. This indicates that the site may have been ritually significant even in pre-Byzantine days. This grotto, behind and below Mary's house, was the site of the Annunciation. A pair of granite columns in the grotto are said to have supernatural powers.

Grotto of the Holy Family

A small deep cave with two small entrances marks the site where, tradition has it, Jesus lived with his mother Mary and where he was

Interior of the Church of Annunciation

brought up. The cave is so low that one must stoop to enter.

Mary's Well

The Church of St. Gabriel

The Church of St. Gabriel stands close by Mary's Well near the fountain head. A 12th century Crusader church was built on this site in tribute to the tradition which states that the Angel Gabriel first appeared to Mary by the well.

The present church was built by the Greek Orthodox in 1781. Today the church has a large congregation composed of the city's Greek Orthodox followers.

The Synagogue

In a courtyard just off the city's main market lane is an ancient hall, 30 feet by 26 feet, noted by Christian pilgrims as early as 570 A.D. Tradition has it that this is the site of the synagogue which Jesus regularly attended on the Sabbath (Luke 4:16).

Mary's Well

Nazareth has known only one spring throughout its history.

An aqueduct brings the spring water to an ornamental fountain located just below St. Gabriel's Church. Here, local boys come with donkeys and clay jars to fetch water just as in Jesus' day.

Luke 1, 26–35:

"In the sixth month the angel Gabriel was sent from God to a city of Galilee named Nazareth, to a virgin betrothed to a man whose name was Joseph, of the house of David: And the virgin's name was Mary. And he came to her and said, "Hail, O favoured one, the Lord is with you!" But she was greatly troubled at the saying, and considered in her mind what sort of greeting this might be. And the angel said to her, "Do not be afraid, Mary, for you have found favour with God. And behold, you will conceive in your womb and bear a son, and you shall call his name Jesus.

He will be great, and will be called the son of the most high; and the Lord God will give to him the throne of his father David, and he will reign over the house of Jacob forever; and of his kingdom there will be no end".

And Mary said to the angel, "How shall this be since I have no husband?"

And the angel said to her, "The Holy Spirit will come upon you, and the power of the most high will overshadow you: Therefore the child to be born will be called Holy, the Son of God."

Cana

Four miles beyond Nazareth in the direction of Tiberias is the Arab village of Cana. The Christian inhabitants, which number half the local population, belong to the Catholic, Greek or Melkite Churches.

Below: The Synagogue
Greek Orthodox Church of the Annunciation

Cana is the scene of two important New Testament happenings. Nathaniel, a native of Cana, was initially quite sceptical of Jesus. It was he who said "can anything good come out of Nazareth?" (John 1:46).

Also here at Cana, Jesus performed his first miracle: at a wedding he was attending, the wine required for the sanctification gave out. Jesus commanded that six stone jars used in the ritual purification be filled with water. When the water was drawn off it miraculously turned to wine. This was to be the first of Jesus' signs.

The Franciscan Church

The Franciscan parish church was built in 1879 on the remains of a 6th century sanctuary. Excavation in 1901 uncovered a mosaic with the following inscription in Aramaic:

Cana, Roman water jug

fashion from the village well. It is a common meeting place where women gather and gossip before carrying home on their heads the containers filled at the well.

Kfar Cana, the Church of the Miracle

Honoured be the memory of Joseph, son of Tanhum, son of Buta, and his sons, who made this mosaic. May it be for them a blessing Amen.

The Water Jar

In the crypt of the Franciscan church at Cana is a pitcher believed to be of the Jewish period and a replica of one of the six original jars mentioned in John 2:6.

Typical Arab Well

In many Arab villages throughout Galilee and Samaria, water is still drawn in the ancient

37

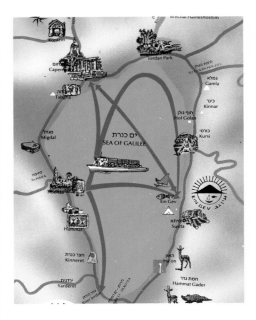

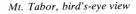
Mount Tabor

Mount Tabor

A lone domed hill stands centred in the northern extension of the Jezreel Valley. Its almost perfectly symmetrical shape plus its seeming aloofness from the surroundings have given Mt. Tabor an air of ritual mystery over the ages. It appears that during Jeroboam's rule a pagan altar was built by Israel on this site (Hos. 5:1). Tabor was the theme of poetic comparison in Jeremy 46:8 and the 88th Psalm, and lay on the border between Issachar and Naphtali.

During the period of the Judges, Barak gathered ten thousand Israelite tribesmen on the slopes of Tabor, while Deborah drew the chariots of Sisera into a muddy trap beneath. The bogged-down Canaanite chariots became easy prey for Barak's manoeuverable forces (Judges 4:4).

For many Christians, Tabor also marks that "high mountain apart" where the Transfiguration of Jesus was viewed by Peter, James and John.

The present day Franciscan Basilica, completed in 1924, is the most recent addition to the succession of churches which have stood on this site since the sixth century. The church with its two storey façade and Byzantine arch was designed after fifth century Roman-Syrian structures.

Mt. Tabor, bird's-eye view

The Sea of Galilee

The focal point of Israel's northcountry is the Sea of Galilee. This harp-shaped fresh water lake is 14 miles long and 7 miles wide. Here, the Holy Land's geography has situated Jesus' first ministry in an elongated trench 480 feet below sea level, for such is the local physical character of the Jordan rift valley where Capernaum, Chorazin, Gergesa and those other sites so important in Christ's early teaching are located. It is only in recent decades that the lush fertility of Galilee's shores with their productive farmland and bustling settlements has been returned to its former biblical state.

The Sea of Galilee is an integral part of Israel's River of Life – the Jordan. The river, having united her three sources Banyas, Hasbani and Dan, about twenty miles to the north, flows into the Sea of Galilee at the northern end and emerges to the south. From here it continues to the Dead Sea.

Each year, the national water carrier pumps 320 million cubic metres of lakewater up into mountain reservoirs; from here, huge conduits carry the water southward to the arid regions of the country. Without the Sea of Galilee's abundant waters for irrigation, the large scale development of Israel's south would have been impossible.

Tiberias

Tiberias on the western shores of the Sea of Galilee was founded by Herod Antipas, Tetrarch of Galilee in 21 A.D. During the city's construction, a Jewish necropolis (cemetery) was uncovered and Jews refused to live there for fear of ritual contamination through contact with the dead. It remained exclusively pagan for many years and we have no evidence that Jesus ever entered the site. Tiberias later became a seat of Jewish scholarship. By the second century the Sanhedrin was located here. It was in Tiberias, that the Mishna and the Jerusalem Talmud were compiled, and Hebrew scriptural punctation was composed.

After serving as the capital of the Galilee during crusader times, Tiberias declined in subsequent centuries. It is currently a growing Jewish city known for its therapeutic hot springs.

Magdala

Nothing but some shrubbery and ruined masonry mark the hometown of Mary Magdalen (Luke 8:2). During the first century A.D. Magdala, also known as Tarichaeae, was a centre for fishing and fish curing, flax weaving and dyeing. Josephus, commander of the Jewish forces in Galilee during the Jewish revolt, fortified this city and from here launched 230 lightly-manned boats in a deceptive attack against Tiberias.

Mt. Arbel

The cliffs of Arbel tower above the plain of Gennesaret along the western shores of the Sea of Galilee. Its cavelined cliffs served as fortified sanctuary for the Maccabees in their battle against the Selucid commander, Bacchides, (I Macc. 9:2) and for the Zealots in their revolt against Herod in 39 B.C. (Josephus, Wars, 1:16) Josephus himself defended these caves against the Romans during the Jewish War of 66–70 A.D. Jesus would have passed beneath these cliffs on his way from Nazareth to Capernaum.

Tiberias, resort hotels along the shore of the Sea of Galilee

The Sea of Galilee, view towards Mt. Arbel from Tabgha

Horns of Hittin

July 5th, 1187, was the darkest day for the Crusader Kingdom of Jerusalem. Here, on the dry, shadeless heights of Hittin, the confident Crusaders went out into battle against the Saracen force headed by Saladin. Cut off from their water supply, roasting in their armour and disrupted by choking brush fires, the Crusader forces broke ranks. Moslem horsemen charged the bewildered enemy and

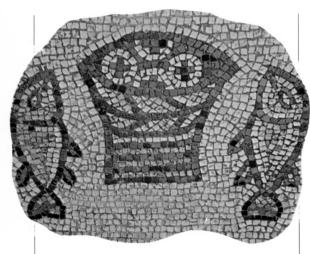

Tabgha, the mosaic of the Loaves and the Fishes

explaining the Greek name for the site, Heptapegon (seven springs). Over the years, the name was distorted to Tabgha. The site of Jesus' miraculous feeding of the multitude is commemorated by a fourth century church whose flower and bird mosaics are the most beautiful in the Holy Land. Between the apse and altar of the church is a fifth to sixth century mosaic, representing fishes and a basket of loaves (Mk. 6:34, Luke 9:10).

Church of St. Peter

St. Peter's church lies close to the site of the multiplication of the loaves. The small church erected by the Franciscans in 1938 was built next to ancient steps leading down to the waterline . Here Jesus revealed himself to the disciples a third time after his crucifixion, as he had promised on the Mt. of Olives (Mt. 26:32). It was here that Jesus told Peter "Feed my lambs, tend my sheep", which has been interpreted as Jesus' bestowal of spiritual supremacy upon Peter over other believers.

The Peaceful Sea of Galilee

Fishing is still a source of income for the inhabitants of the region, though not on the scale of biblical times. The most common fish is St. Peter's fish, or Tilapia Galilea, which is cooked to delicate perfection at many seaside restaurants in Tiberias, and at Kibbutz Ein Gev on the opposite shore.

The Mount of Beatitudes

On a hill rising behind Tabgha is a round chapel built in 1937 and maintained by the Franciscan Sisters. This site, which offers one of Israel's most beautiful panoramas, is where Jesus delivered his Sermon on the Mount.

annihilated them. The Crusaders did not recover from this crushing defeat; it was the beginning of the end of the Latin Kingdom of Jerusalem.

Valley of Ginossar

The Vale of Ginossar (Land of Gennesaret) is a rich plain stretching five miles along the western coast of the Sea of Galilee. Several perennial springs water the vale giving it its natural richness. This plain was often visited by Jesus (Mark 6, 53) and lay on the route leading down to the lake from Nazareth. The modern village of Migdal and the beautiful kibbutz Ginossar now stand on the site described by Josephus as a sub-tropical paradise with a year-round growing season.

Tabgha

The curved northwest shore of the Sea of Galilee contains several brackish springs, thus

The valley of Ginossar seen from Arbel

Tabgha, the Church of St. Peter

The Mount of Beatitudes

Chorazin, ruins of the ancient synagogue

Blessed are the poor in spirit, for theirs is the
   Kingdom of heaven.
Blessed are those who mourn, for they shall be
   comforted.
Blessed are the meek, for they shall inherit the
   earth.
Blessed are those who hunger and thirst for
   righteousness, for they shall be
   satisfied.
Blessed are the merciful, for they shall obtain
   mercy.
Blessed are the pure in heart, for they shall see
   God.
Blessed are the peacemakers, for they shall be
   called the sons of God.
Blessed are those who are persecuted for
   righteousness sake, for theirs is the
   Kingdom of Heaven.

Matthew 5:3–10

Chorazin

"Woe to you, Chorazin" was a curse
pronounced by Jesus on this Galilean village,
as a punishment for its villagers' failure to
follow the teachings of Jesus (Matt 11:21).
Today its ruins can be seen scattered among
the thistles two miles north of Capernaum. The
third century synagogue (above right) was
constructed from local basalt and contains
many interesting carvings, including one of
Medusa. This village was famous for its wheat
during Jesus' time.

Capernaum

Capernaum at the time of Jesus was a border
village between Herod Antipas' Tetrarchy of
Galilee and Hellenistic Gaulanitis. It contained
a customs house, and was garrisoned by a
small Roman detachment. It was here that
Jesus came to teach after his failure to
evangelize Nazareth, and Capernaum became
the centre of his Galilean ministry. Jesus
gathered together his disciples here (Matt.
4,14) and performed many cures (Mk. 1,21; 2,
3, Luke 7, 2).
Today can be seen the remains of a synagogue
2–3 centuries younger than that in which Jesus
taught, though most likely on the same site.
The main material used for building is
well-dressed and carved limestone. The
synagogue is typical of the basilica style of the

*The Star of David, detail of the Capernaum
synagogue*

41

Capernaum, general view of the ancient Synagogue and the excavations

period, with Corinthian columns. Nearby are the remains of an octagonal structure, thought to be built on the remains of Peter's house. Beneath can be seen some of the stone artifacts of ancient Capernaum: a carved palm tree, mill stone and the star of David.

Gergesa (Kursi)

On the eastern shores of the Sea of Galilee in the pagan Decapolis. Jesus exorcized the

Gergesa (Kursi), ruins of the ancient church

unclean spirits from the possessed man who lived like a madman among the tombs.
And when he saw Jesus he ran and worshipped him; and crying out with a loud voice, he said, 'What have you to do with me, Jesus, Son of the Most High God.' For he said to him 'Come out of the man, you unclean spirit' and Jesus asked him, 'What is your name?' He replied, 'My name is Legion; for we are many.'
Jesus then allowed the unclean spirits to come out and enter a herd of two thousand swine, who plunged down headlong into the sea and drowned.

The Galilee boat

The Galilee Boat

This ancient boat was discovered at low tide in the Sea of Galilee during the drought year of 1985 and is believed to be a fisherman's boat dating back to 70–20 B.C.

The River Jordan

The southern continuation of the Jordan River extends 65 miles from the Sea of Galilee to the Dead Sea. A slow, shallow stream, the Jordan meanders in its channel, overgrown on both banks by sub-tropical trees and tangled bush. This is the jungle of the Jordan referred to by Jeremiah as inhabited by lions (Jer. 49:19). The stream is 60–100 feet wide and varies in depth from 3–12 feet.

The Jordan's egress from the Sea of Galilee (right) is one of the few places along the length of the river which is accessible to visitors today, and is a common site for prayer and baptism.

Yardenit

Yardenit is today a popular site for baptism of pilgrims to the Holy Land. Situated close to where the Jordan leaves the Sea of Galilee, it boasts modern facilities including showers and a restaurant.

The Jordan valley, southern edge of the Sea of Galilee

Yardenit, the site of baptism

The Jordan Valley

Travelling south from the Sea of Galilee, one enters a rich maze of fertile fields. Irrigation and hard work have converted this once barren, malarial plain into one of Israel's most fertile areas. The foremost and oldest of Israeli Kibbutzim – Degania (founded in 1911) – is located here.

The cleft in the mountains to the east is the valley of the Yarmuk River, which runs into the Jordan some five miles south of the Sea of Galilee. This cleft separates the Golan Heights from the hills of Gilead in Transjordan.

Hazor, the entrance to the water system

Hazor

This important biblical site was a Canaanite stronghold during the time of the Israelite conquest, and a fortified barrier against northern invasion during the Kingdom of Israel. The mound consists of two parts: a higher, more strongly defended acropolis, 40 acres in size, and a lower city covering 150 acres and protected by a beaten earth rampart.

The River Jordan and snow-covered Mt. Hermon

Joshua captured and burnt Hazor in the 13th century B.C., yet the city must have recovered quickly, for Jabin, King of Hazor, set his forces against Deborah (Judges 4:2). It was fortified by Solomon (I Kings 9:15). The pillared ruins above are part of a storehouse built by the House of Omri in the 9th century B.C. The city was destroyed by the Assyrian king Tiglath-Pileser in 732 B.C.
Of special interest are the town's siegeproof water system, and the museum located at the adjacent kibbutz, Ayelet Hashahar.

The Sources of the River Jordan

Mount Hermon is Israel's largest watershed. The spring snow thawing from her summit charges the two fountainheads, Dan and Banias, which are the Jordan's greatest sources. A third Jordan tributary, the Hasbani, flows down from Lebanon.

Caesaria Phillipi

Caesaria Phillipi at the base of Mt. Hermon stands at the headwaters of one of the sources of the Jordan. Its present name is Banias, a corruption of the Greek word Paneas, for here stood a shrine to the god Pan. Here Herod the Great built a shrine to Caesar. Phillipi his son, embellished the town and named it Caesaria. Caesaria Phillipi is to be distinguished from the Herodean port-city Caesaria Maritima.
It was here that Simon acknowledged Jesus as the Messiah, to which Jesus replied "You are Peter, and on this rock (Petra) I will build my church, and the powers of death shall not prevail against it."

Safed

The picturesque alleyways, colorful sunsets, crisp mountain air and mystical setting make Safed, in the northern Galilee, one of Israel's most popular holiday resorts.
Many of Israel's foremost artists have settled here and their galleries are always open to the interested art fan. The painters and sculptors

Banias, Caesaria Phillipi

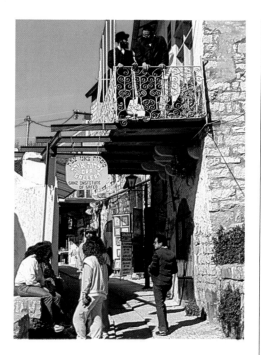

Safed, lane in the old city

Acre

Acre is first mentioned in the Egyptian excration texts in the 19th century B.C. From the 25th to the 13th centuries B.C., it was a large important Canaanite city. Though part of the inheritance of Asher, it never seems to have been conquered by the Israelites (Judges 1:31). In the 7th and 8th centures B.C., it was an important Phoenician city. It flourished as a Hellenistic city under the name Ptolemais. Here, Paul disembarked (Acts 21:7). The city is mentioned once in the New Testament. Acre entered its most glorious period with the coming of the Crusaders. It was taken by Baldwin I in 1104, and became a chief stronghold of the Crusader Kingdom. After the disastrous Christian defeat at Hittin in 1187, the city surrendered to Saladin without resistance but was soon reinforced by knights from all over Europe, only to fall in 1191. During the following century, St. Joan de Acre became capital of the Latin Kingdom. Rivalry between the principal chivalrous orders and corruption within the merchant population weakened the city's strength and hastened its fall to the Moslems in 1291.

Acre, ancient Turkish cannon

draw much of their inspiration from the city's importance as one of Judaism's sacred cities of the Middle Ages. Under the guidance of a 16th century charismatic Jewish sage, Rabbi Isaac Luria, Safed became a centre for Kaballism and a renaissance of scholarly activity in the Holy Land. At this time an unsuccessful attempt was made to reconstitute the Sanhedrin. Here, Rabbi Joseph Caro wrote the *"Shulhan Aruch"*, a comprehensive collection of Jewish laws and ritual.

Bird's eye view of Acre

Many Crusader buildings and fortifications ramain intact to this day. The Acre Mosque was built by the notorious 18th century Moslem ruler, Jazzar Pasha and is among the most important mosques in Israel.

Rosh Hanikra

Rosh Hanikra is a group of beautiful natural grottos formed by wave action against the chalk cliffs on Israel's Lebanese frontier. A cable-car enables visitors to descend in to the grottos at water level. A railroad tunnel, now sealed, can be seen in the centre of the photo. This was part of the former railroad link between Palestine and Lebanon, built during the British Mandate.

Ladder of Tyre

Israel's long sandy coast stretches northward to the white chalk cliffs of the Ladder of Tyre on the Lebanese frontier. The abandoned Arab vilage of e-Zib stands on the waterfront. Nearby, is the kibbutz Gesher Haziv, a "Club Mediterranean" resort and a youth hostel.

The white cliffs of Rosh Hanikra and the grotto

Haifa

Haifa is Israel's third largest city, after Tel Aviv and Jerusalem. The city stretches from the shores of the best naturally sheltered bay on Israel's Mediterranean coast, up the slopes and onto the summit of Mt. Carmel's northwestern tip.

Three factors contributed to Haifa's growth as the country's chief northern city: the construction of the Hejaz rail line in 1905, of the modern harbour in 1933, and the refineries in 1934.

Haifa does not appear in the Bible and its name is first mentioned in Talmudic commentaries of the third century.

The city was destroyed by the Crusader Tancred, but was rebuilt and fortified in the 18th century by the Beduin ruler, Taher el Omer.

From the Carmel, above the city, a panorama of Haifa and the whole western Galilee is revealed (above). The outstanding features to be seen from here are the gold-domed Bahai Temple, the busy harbour with ships waiting outside the breakwater for their turn to unload, the red roofed houses of the former German Templar Colony and the large Dagon grain silo skirting the dockside.

The Baha'i Shrines

Haifa is the world centre of the Bahai faith. The neo-classical archives and gold-domed shrine are situated in one of Israel's most beautiful garden estates. In 1844, a Persian, Mirza Mohammed Ali Mohammad declared himself the forerunner, or "El Bab" and proclaimed the imminent coming of the awaited Mahdi. In 1866, a follower, Baha Ulla, announced that he was the awaited one. The Turks banished Baha Ulla to Acre, where he is buried. The Bahai faith preaches continual revelation and respects all previous enlightened teachings. The sect now numbers over two million. The gold-domed shrine contains the remains of both el Bab and the Baha Ulla's successor, Abdul Basha.

Opposite: view of Haifa from Mt. Carmel River Kishon and Mt. Carmel

The Stella Maris Monastery

The Carmelite Monastery of Stella Maris is
perched high atop Mt. Carmel's promentory,
overlooking the Mediterranean. Under the
church's high altar is a cave in which Elijah is
said to have dwelt while taking refuge from
Ahab. Jewish tradition, however, places the
site of refuge in a cave further down the slope.
During Napoleon's siege of Acre in 1799, the
monastery was used as a hospital for wounded
French soldiers. Outside the church stands a
small pyramid over the remains of those
wounded soldiers massacred by the Turks
during the French retreat.

The Carmelite order was established here by
Berthold of Limoges during Crusader times.

Mount Carmel

Mount Carmel is the seaward extension of the
Samaria range. It stretches along fourteen
miles and is 3–4 miles wide, jutting across the
coastal plain to meet the sea at Haifa.

Carmel was extolled by the prophets for its
beauty and fertility (Songs 7:5, Isa. 35:2, Amos
1:2) and as a place of worship and retreat (I
Kings 18:19, II Kings 2:25, Amos 9:3). Today
the mountain is covered with oak and carob
groves with several settlements scattered on its
broad rolling plateau. In biblical times this
plateau was heavily cultivated. A number of
villages here, Daliat el Carmel and Isafiya are
inhabited by a non Moslem Arab people called
the Druze. This sect broke with formal Islam
in the 11th century and was founded by Ismael
al Darazi. Druze settlements are scattered in
Lebanon, Galilee, Carmel and the Golan
heights.

Monastery of Elijah

On the southeastern heights of Carmel,
overlooking the plain of Jezreel, is the site of
Elijah's contest with the priests of Baal, to
prove who was the true and living God.
Compare Elijah's altar (I Kings 18:31, Ex. 21:
25–26) with the Canaanite altar shown in the
section on Megiddo. After god's fiery
acceptance of Elijah's drenched sacrifice, the
prophet slayed the priest of Baal in the brook
Kishon, some 1550 feet below. The statue of
Elijah stands in the grounds of the Carmelite
Monastery of Elijah.

Stella Maris Monastery, Haifa

Elijah's monument, Mukhraka, Mt. Carmel

The Stella Maris Monastery

The Carmelite Monastery of Stella Maris is perched high atop Mt. Carmel's promentory, overlooking the Mediterranean. Under the church's high altar is a cave in which Elijah is said to have dwelt while taking refuge from Ahab. Jewish tradition, however, places the site of refuge in a cave further down the slope. During Napoleon's siege of Acre in 1799, the monastery was used as a hospital for wounded French soldiers. Outside the church stands a small pyramid over the remains of those wounded soldiers massacred by the Turks during the French retreat.

The Carmelite order was established here by Berthold of Limoges during Crusader times.

Mount Carmel

Mount Carmel is the seaward extension of the Samaria range. It stretches along fourteen miles and is 3–4 miles wide, jutting across the coastal plain to meet the sea at Haifa.

Carmel was extolled by the prophets for its beauty and fertility (Songs 7:5, Isa. 35:2, Amos 1:2) and as a place of worship and retreat (I Kings 18:19, II Kings 2:25, Amos 9:3). Today the mountain is covered with oak and carob groves with several settlements scattered on its broad rolling plateau. In biblical times this plateau was heavily cultivated. A number of villages here, Daliat el Carmel and Isafiya are inhabited by a non Moslem Arab people called the Druze. This sect broke with formal Islam in the 11th century and was founded by Ismael al Darazi. Druze settlements are scattered in Lebanon, Galilee, Carmel and the Golan heights.

Monastery of Elijah

On the southeastern heights of Carmel, overlooking the plain of Jezreel, is the site of Elijah's contest with the priests of Baal, to prove who was the true and living God. Compare Elijah's altar (I Kings 18:31, Ex. 21:25–26) with the Canaanite altar shown in the section on Megiddo. After god's fiery acceptance of Elijah's drenched sacrifice, the prophet slayed the priest of Baal in the brook Kishon, some 1550 feet below. The statue of Elijah stands in the grounds of the Carmelite Monastery of Elijah.

Stella Maris Monastery, Haifa

Elijah's monument, Mukhraka, Mt. Carmel